Symbols of American Freedom

The Washington Monument

by Julia Schaffer

Series Consultant: Jerry D. Thompson,
Regents Professor of History,
Texas A&M International University

CHELSEA CLUBHOUSE

An Imprint of Chelsea House Publishers

Symbols of American Freedom: The Washington Monument

Copyright ©2010 by Infobase Publishing

Chelsea Clubhouse
An imprint of Chelsea House Publishers
132 West 31st Street
New York NY 10001

Library of Congress Cataloging-in-Publication Data
Schaffer, Julia.
        The Washington Monument / by Julia Schaffer.
              p. cm. — (Symbols of American freedom)
        Includes index.
        ISBN 978-1-60413-517-6
        1. Washington Monument (Washington, D.C.)—Juvenile literature. 2. Washington, George, 1732-1799—Monuments—Washington (D.C.)—Juvenile literature. 3. Washington (D.C.)—Buildings, structures, etc.—Juvenile literature. I. Title. II. Series.
     F203.4.W3S34 2010
     975.3—dc22   2009013482

Chelsea Clubhouse books are available at special discounts when purchased in bulk quantities for businesses, associations, institutions, or sales promotions. Please call our Special Sales Department in New York at (212) 967-8800 or (800) 322-8755.

You can find Chelsea Clubhouse on the World Wide Web at http://www.chelseahouse.com

Developed for Chelsea House by RJF Publishing LLC (www.RJFpublishing.com)
Text and cover design by Tammy West/Westgraphix LLC
Maps by Stefan Chabluk
Photo research by Edward A. Thomas
Index by Nila Glikin

Photo Credits: 5: Index Stock Imagery/Photolibrary; 6: Guenter Fischer/Photolibrary; 7: Private Collection/ Peter Newark American Pictures/The Bridgeman Art Library; 9, 35: National Park Service; 13, 25, 29, 39: © North Wind/North Wind Picture Archives; 14: Library of Congress LC-DIG-pga-01370; 15: Private Collection/Photo © Boltin Picture Library/The Bridgeman Art Library; 17: Private Collection/The Bridgeman Art Library; 18: National Army Museum, London/The Bridgeman Art Library; 21: Library of Congress LC-USZC2-3052; 23: House of Representatives, Washington, D.C./The Bridgeman Art Library; 27: Smithsonian Institution, Washington, D.C./The Bridgeman Art Library; 31, 41: AP/Wide World Photos; 32: Library of Congress; 36: Library of Congress LC-USZ62-59908; 43: © William Phillips/Alamy.

Printed and bound in the United States of America

Bang RJF 10 9 8 7 6 5 4 3 2 1

Note: Quotations in the text are used essentially as originally written. In some cases, spelling, punctuation, and the like have been modernized to aid student understanding.

Table of Contents

Words that are defined in the Glossary are in **bold** type
the first time they appear in the text.

Chapter 1

The Importance of the Washington Monument

I n the winter of 1799, thousands of Americans dressed in black. Stores sold out of black fabric for six months. Why were so many people wearing black? They were **mourning** the death of George Washington. He was the first president of the new country, the United States of America. He was also the general who helped Americans win a war for their freedom: the American Revolution.

Washington was described as honest, modest, and brave. He was also called dignified and commanding. He had many of the traits that Americans valued most. Some people wanted to build a **monument** for him. They had the idea while he was still alive. After he died, even more people wanted to build something for him. They wanted to show how much they admired him. They wanted to show they were grateful to him.

Finally, after many years, a monument was built that was more than 555 feet (169 meters)

Surrounded by flags, the Washington Monument stands in the city of
Washington, D.C., and is one of the city's most popular sites to visit.

high. It was constructed in the heart of the nation's **capital**, Washington, D.C. At the time, the Washington Monument was the tallest human-made structure in the world. More than 100 years had gone by from the time people first thought of building it until it was finished. First, a design for the monument had to be chosen. Then, money had to be raised in order to build it. People also had to figure out how to safely build something that would be so tall.

Tributes to Washington

All over the United States, there are places and objects named for George Washington. There is the country's capital city, Washington, D.C. There is the state of Washington. Thirty-one states have counties named for him. There are also many bridges, roads, schools, and colleges with his name. Take a look at a one dollar bill. You will find Washington's face on it. Can you find something named Washington near where you live?

George Washington University in Washington, D.C., is named for the first president, and a sculpture of George Washington is outside one of the entrances to the school.

What They Said About Him

When George Washington died, everyone had good things to say about him. Henry Lee was a **representative** to the U.S. **Congress** from Virginia. After Washington's death, Lee wrote that Washington was, "First in war, first in peace, first in the hearts of his countrymen." That summed up how many Americans felt. To them, Washington was first and best in every category.

Honoring George Washington

Today, the monument is a familiar sight in Washington, D.C. It is also a popular stop for people sightseeing in the city. About 600,000 visitors come every year to honor George Washington and to see the view from the top of the monument.

This book tells the history of the monument from the first idea for a design to the last stone placed on top. It also tells how a boy growing up in the British **colony** of Virginia became a great American hero. That boy was named George Washington.

This painting shows George Washington when he was the leader of the American army in the American Revolution.

Chapter 2

George Washington's Early Years

George Washington was born in Westmoreland County, Virginia, on February 22, 1732. He had two older half brothers and an older half sister. Soon, he had five younger brothers and sisters, too. George and his family moved three times when he was a boy. First they lived in a four-room house. Then they moved to an **estate** that would later be called Mount Vernon. After that, they moved to a third farm. All three locations were in the British colony of Virginia.

When George was 11, his father died. His father left him the family farm. George was expected to help his mother run it. He had been planning to go to school in Britain, which his older brothers had done. Now, however, George was needed at home. His education was a mix of schoolwork and farm work. In school, he studied math, geography, and astronomy. In the fields, he learned how to grow tobacco, raise animals, and **survey** land.

As a teenager, George Washington worked as a surveyor, getting the chance to travel to western Virginia and learn how to survive in the wilderness.

Mount Vernon was his favorite place to spend time. That was where his brother Lawrence lived. George looked up to his brother. Lawrence had fought for the British military. George wanted to do the same. When he had the chance to join the British Navy, though, his mother begged him not to. George's bags were already packed, but he unpacked them and stayed home. Instead, he had a different adventure. He visited the American **frontier**.

Surveying the Land

At this time, the British colonies were expanding. There was land to be settled to the west. Surveyors were needed to measure the land and mark the boundaries. George joined a team doing this work in the Shenandoah Valley in western Virginia. At the age of 16, he took a 31-day trip over the Blue Ridge Mountains and into the frontier. It was farther from home than he had ever gone.

Along the way, George had new experiences. He got to swim horses across a river. He met Native Americans of different tribes. He also had to sleep on a bed full of lice and other bugs.

After that trip, George kept working as a surveyor. He traveled in the woods and visited settlements. At times, he faced danger from wild animals, harsh weather, and even other people. He learned how to live under tough conditions. It was a skill he would need later in his life.

Between trips, George spent time with Lawrence and his wife and her family. He joined them for dinners and dances. All this ended when Lawrence got sick with a disease called tuberculosis. George went with him to the British colony of Barbados. They hoped the warm weather there would make Lawrence better, but it did not. Lawrence died in 1752.

Smallpox

When George and Lawrence were in Barbados, George also caught a dangerous disease. George got smallpox. Unlike many other people who got the disease, George recovered. This proved to be important years later when he was fighting in the American Revolution. Thousands of soldiers died of smallpox, but Washington did not. He had already had the disease. Because of this, he was safe.

The Start of a Military Career

George applied for Lawrence's old job as head of the Virginia **militia**. That job was too big for him. He knew how to travel through the frontier, but he had no military experience. He was given a different position. He was put in charge of part of the militia. Soon, he had his first assignment.

Beyond the British colonies was valuable land. The land lay in an area called the Ohio Valley. The British and the French both wanted to own the land. Native Americans—who had lived there longer than either side—were split over which side to support.

In 1753, the British governor of Virginia sent George on a mission into the Ohio Valley. He told George to give a letter to the French, telling them to get out of the area. The French were already building forts in an area claimed by Virginia.

George left in October with a fur trader as his guide. He also got help from a Native American chief. George delivered the letter, but the

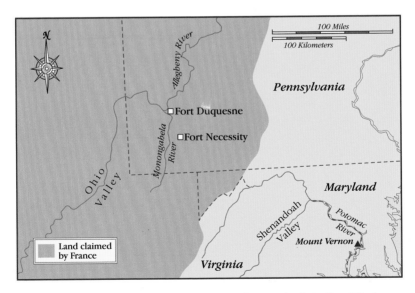

A few years after surveying land in the Shenandoah Valley, Washington led militia troops into what is now western Pennsylvania and fought a French force at Fort Necessity.

11

French would not back down. They said they were going to stay in the Ohio Valley. George rushed back to Virginia to deliver the news. The trip home was difficult. George and his guide both fell off a raft into a river filled with ice.

Fighting the French

The governor sent George back again in 1754. He told him to take 159 men and build a fort where the Allegheny and the Monongahela rivers come together, near where the city of Pittsburgh, Pennsylvania, is today.

George and his men began the trek. They carried heavy cannons, food, and weapons through the wilderness, but they never reached their destination. They changed their plans when they learned that the French had already set up a fort, called Fort Duquesne, at the same spot. George and his men made a surprise attack on a smaller group of French soldiers. They killed the leader of the group.

George did not have enough men to attack Fort Duquesne. He had 159 men, and the French had 1,000. George told his men to build a fort and wait for help to arrive. The fort was named Fort Necessity, because out of necessity the soldiers had to build it to protect themselves. More men arrived, but George's troops were still outnumbered when the French attacked. The French won. They allowed George and his men to leave alive. They demanded, however, that George sign a paper admitting that he had killed a French leader who was on a peaceful mission. The incident marked the start of a conflict known as the French and Indian War, which lasted until 1763. George returned home to Virginia.

New Responsibilities

George knew he could be a better military leader if he had the skills of a British officer. He had no formal training and neither did the men he was leading. George wanted to learn from well-trained British fighters. He soon got his chance.

The British king was determined to win the Ohio Valley. He assigned a British general, Edward Braddock, and two regiments of professional soldiers to take over Fort Duquesne. George offered to help them find their way. This force was attacked before it reached the fort. French soldiers and Native Americans fighting with the French surprised the British in the woods. The two sides fought a bloody battle in which about 1,000 British soldiers died. Their leader, General Braddock, died too. George was lucky to remain alive. Bullets flew past him. Two horses were shot while he rode them. His clothes were torn by bullets.

Now the French and the Native Americans fighting with them got bold. They began attacking small Virginia towns. They stole goods and frightened the settlers. George was put in charge of defending 350 miles of the Virginia frontier. Once again, his soldiers were untrained. George held this job for three years.

By then, the British were ready to try again to take Fort Duquesne. They

British soldiers led by General Edward Braddock were attacked and defeated by French troops and their Indian allies in one of the battles for control of the Ohio Valley.

Martha Washington (1731–1802)

Martha Washington was born in Virginia in 1731. When she was 18, she married Daniel Parke Custis. Martha and Daniel had four children. Two of them died when they were just a few years old. Daniel was a wealthy man. He was also 20 years older than Martha. When he died in 1757, Martha inherited his wealth. As a widow, she raised her two surviving children and managed her estate. She met George Washington while he was home between trips to the Ohio Valley. They were married in 1759 in a ceremony at her home. Martha was known for being energetic and friendly. When George was serving as a general, she organized entertainment for soldiers at their winter camps. When George was president, she hosted guests every week. She was also devoted to her family. Martha died in 1802 at the age of 70.

brought 6,000 soldiers into the Ohio Valley. George was part of the group. Outnumbered, the French escaped before the British arrived. George came home after this victory. He decided he was finished with the military. He had a big estate to care for, and he was about to get married. He was 27 years old.

Life at Mount Vernon

George married Martha Custis in 1759. He also adopted her children, Jacky and Patsy, who were four and two years old. At this time, George was a representative in Virginia's **legislature**. It was called the House of

This painting shows Mount Vernon at the time George Washington lived there.

Burgesses. Most of his energy, however, went into farming. George had inherited Mount Vernon from Lawrence. He also got more land when he married Martha. Now he expanded Mount Vernon. He wanted to make it a great farm.

George farmed six days a week. He grew tobacco and wheat. He bred cattle. He had peach and apple orchards. George learned how to grow different crops to keep the soil healthy. He loved life as a farmer.

George's farm relied on slaves. They worked in the fields for no money. They also lived on the farm. They were considered the property of the Washington family. At this time, slavery was legal, but George doubted whether it was right. As he got older, he became more and more convinced that slavery was wrong.

Among the 13 American colonies, there were different ideas about slavery. Some people thought it should remain legal. Some thought it should be outlawed. For most of their history, the colonies had operated separately. That was about to change.

General and President

Great Britain needed to pay its **debts** from the French and Indian War, so the king raised taxes on the colonies. This made many American colonists angry. They refused to buy goods that were taxed. In Boston, Massachusetts, they dumped British tea into the harbor. Then the British government got much tougher. It said the Americans could not rule their own colonies. In Virginia, it tried to shut down the House of Burgesses. Now, the 13 colonies needed to work together to fight back.

Representatives from 12 of the 13 colonies met in Philadelphia, Pennsylvania, in 1774. This meeting was called the First Continental Congress. George Washington was one of the representatives from Virginia. The Continental Congress met again beginning in May 1775. By the time this Second Continental Congress began, fighting between the colonists and British troops had already taken place. The colonies needed to choose a commander to help them fight against the British. They chose Washington for the job.

He worried that he did not have the experience to lead an entire army and said that in Congress. Still, he accepted the job. He said, though, that he did not want to be paid. He knew the colonies did not have much money. Washington returned home to Mount Vernon. Then he traveled to Boston to take command of the army. The American Revolution had begun. General Washington was commander in chief.

Leader in the American Revolution

Washington was not impressed with the soldiers he had to lead. They were untrained and often drunk. Fortunately, he had experience leading untrained fighters. Washington's army drove the British out of Boston. Then they raced south to defend New York City. That proved to be much harder, though.

Angry over the British tax on tea, colonists in Boston, dressed as Native Americans, dumped boxes of British tea into the harbor.

The Battles of Lexington and Concord

The first shots in the American Revolution were fired in Massachusetts in April 1775. The militia there had learned that the British Army was planning to capture their weapons. These were being stored in the town of Concord, near Boston. Members of the militia were told to be ready to fight back when the British arrived. The British troops stopped first in the nearby town of Lexington. No one knows which side shot first, but a battle began. Members of the militia were outnumbered. Then, the British went on to Concord. There, it was the militia forces that were larger and stronger. They chased the British back to Boston, gathering more men as they went.

This painting shows the first shots of the American Revolution being fired at Lexington between American militia troops and British soldiers.

Washington's army lost badly in New York, including in the battles of Long Island and White Plains. Thousands of American soldiers were killed. Washington and his remaining men had to escape to New Jersey. Then, they crossed the Delaware River to Pennsylvania.

The British thought they were about to win the war. Many Americans thought so, too. Washington needed to turn things around. He knew the strengths and weaknesses of the British

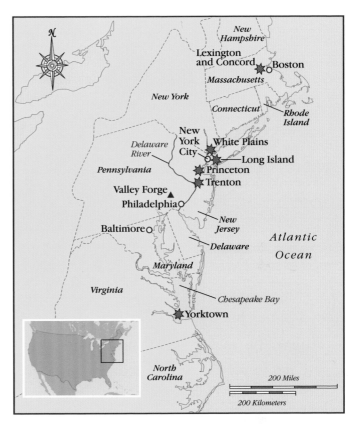

Washington let the American army in several major battles in New York and New Jersey—and then in the American victory at Yorktown that ensured independence.

Army. He thought his best strategy was to stage a surprise attack. That is what he did in December 1776.

On Christmas night, Washington led 2,400 soldiers through a driving snowstorm. In the dark of the night, they boarded boats at the edge of the Delaware River. The river was clogged with ice, but they managed to cross into New Jersey. They marched 10 miles (16 kilometers) through the snow and surprised the enemy soldiers in Trenton just as they were waking up. The Americans won in about two hours. They did it without losing any of their soldiers.

Declaring Independence

In the summer of 1776, members of the Continental Congress drafted a Declaration of Independence. This document announced the formation of the United States of America. This was a new nation independent of Britain. The Declaration was written by Thomas Jefferson of Virginia. He later became an adviser to George Washington and the third president of the United States. The Declaration of Independence was approved on July 4. A few days later, it was read out loud to Washington's soldiers in New York. They cheered in celebration. Some of them destroyed a statue of King George III of Great Britain. They melted it down and made bullets.

The British planned to attack back in January 1777. They were going to surprise the American camp, but Washington guessed their plan. He marched his soldiers out of their camp during the night. He left their fires burning in order to trick the British. Then he surprised the British by attacking in Princeton. It was another victory for Washington's army.

Americans began to believe they could win the war. Young men signed up to fight. But 1777 was not a good year for Washington's army. The British captured a major city, Philadelphia. Washington's army camped west of the city in Valley Forge, Pennsylvania, for the winter of 1777–1778. It was a terrible winter. Many soldiers had no shoes or coats. No one had enough food. Until they built cabins, they slept in freezing tents. Some 2,000 soldiers died from cold, starvation, and diseases such as smallpox.

Victory at Yorktown

In the spring of 1778, the French government decided to help the Americans. France sent troops to fight with the colonists. In 1781, a French commander suggested that American and French forces surprise the British forces in eastern Virginia, near Chesapeake Bay. Washington pretended he was going to invade Staten Island, New York. He told this to people he knew were British spies. He even told his own soldiers. When it came time to move, he marched his troops down to the British fort at Yorktown, Virginia. The French Navy blocked the British from sailing out of Chesapeake Bay. The British Army was surrounded and trapped. On October 19, the British general, Charles Cornwallis, surrendered to General Washington.

The Battle of Yorktown was the last large battle of the American Revolution. Now it was time to make a peace treaty. That took two more years. The Treaty of Paris that officially ended the war—and in which Great Britain officially recognized American independence—was signed in 1783.

In early 1783 (even before the peace treaty was signed) the American government decided to send its soldiers home. The soldiers wanted to be

This picture shows British officers surrendering to the victorious American army at the Battle of Yorktown.

paid first. The government had little money at this time. It offered the soldiers papers saying that they would be paid later. This made the soldiers angry. After all, they had risked their lives in the war. They talked about rebelling. Washington convinced them not to. The soldiers said goodbye to their commander and went home peacefully.

Problems for the New Nation

Washington returned to Mount Vernon. The estate was in bad shape after the war. He put his energy into fixing it. He worried, however, about the United States. The new country was having problems.

In 1781, the Continental Congress had adopted a document called the Articles of Confederation. In this document the 13 colonies—now 13 states—set up a national government for the new United States of America. Under the Articles, states were given a lot of power. Little power was given to the national, or **federal**, government. The federal government could not force citizens to pay taxes. It could not give away land or take responsibility for unpaid debts.

The Articles of Confederation gave the federal government some power, such as the power to conduct foreign relations and declare war. From Washington's point of view, the federal government needed more power. During the war, the army had needed money for supplies, but some states did not pay as much as they said they would. The federal government had no way to make them pay. As a result, the army suffered. Washington knew this. He had seen his troops go with too little food and ammunition. Now Washington wanted to make the federal government stronger.

Writing a Constitution

Washington supported the idea of a meeting, or convention, of all 13 states. The original purpose of the meeting was to make changes in the Articles of Confederation to improve it. But in the end, the delegates at the meeting decided to write a new **constitution** that would replace the Articles of Confederation. This new U.S. Constitution would make the federal government stronger. Washington agreed to go to the Constitutional Convention. He also agreed to be in charge of (chair) the meeting.

The meeting took place in Philadelphia in 1787. It lasted four months. The weather was very hot, but the delegates worked in a room with all of the windows closed. They did not want other people to hear what they were discussing until the whole Constitution was ready.

When the Constitution was finally finished, Washington supported it. He hoped that others would too. He feared that without it, the country would fall apart. Washington wrote to his fellow Virginian, Patrick Henry.

Washington (standing at right in this painting) led the convention in 1787 that wrote a new constitution for the new nation.

The President Sets Precedents

As president, Washington faced questions that had never been answered before. How does a president behave? What is the president called? Should he be called "your Highness"? Washington asked to be called "Mr. President." He wanted to be sure he was making wise choices. He knew that every choice he made would set a **precedent** (an example for the future). In a letter to his friend James Madison, he wrote that he wished these precedents would be "fixed on true principles."

He urged him to support the new Constitution, writing: "It or disunion is before us to choose from." Eventually, all the states approved the Constitution.

The Constitution made the federal government stronger. It also created a new job: president of the United States. Representatives from the states were named to an Electoral College. This group was given the power to choose the president. In February 1789, they chose Washington. Washington had not asked for the job, but he accepted it.

President Washington

Washington was **inaugurated** in New York City on April 30, 1789. As president, he led a country of 4 million people. The country had very little money and a lot of debt from the war. Washington also faced other challenges. He had to make sure that the new nation survived.

Washington told his advisers he would resign at the end of his first term. They protested. They wanted him to stay on as president. They said there was still too much arguing between the states. They said that only Washington could hold the country together. He agreed to run for a second term, and he was reelected in 1792.

George Washington was sworn in as the first president of the United States in 1789.

At this time, France and Great Britain were at war again. Washington believed it was important not to choose sides. He wanted to show the independence of the United States. He made a **Neutrality** Proclamation that said that the United States would not help either country in the war.

When he had time, Washington visited northern and southern states. He wanted to see how people lived in different places. He also wanted to see whether citizens supported the federal government. In general, he found that they did. People did not support the government, however, when it came to some decisions.

To pay off the government's debts, a tax was placed on whiskey. Farmers in Pennsylvania got angry. They made money from selling whiskey. They did not want to pay a tax. A group of them attacked a tax collector near Pittsburgh. They cut off his hair and covered him in tar and feathers. Other farmers fired gunshots. They talked about putting together their own army or even starting a new country. Washington sent a warning for them to stop. Then, he organized a militia to fight them if necessary. In the end, the rebels gave in without fighting. This event—which was called the Whiskey Rebellion—gave Washington the chance to use the new powers of the federal government.

Stepping Down as President

Washington was asked to run for a third term as president. This time, he refused. In doing so, he set one more important precedent. Washington

In Their Own Words

Washington's Farewell Address

Washington's "farewell address" in 1797 was not a speech. It was actually a letter that was printed in newspapers throughout the United States. In his farewell, Washington warned Americans not to let the country be split apart by political differences or regional loyalties. He urged them to work hard to uphold the union between the states. He ended on a personal note. He said:

"I anticipate with pleasing expectation…the sweet enjoyment of partaking, in the midst of my fellow-citizens, the benign influence of good laws under a free government…the happy reward, I trust, of our mutual cares, labors, and dangers."

Guests brought Washington gifts and good wishes when he celebrated his birthday at Mount Vernon in 1798. Martha is standing at his side.

made it clear that presidents, unlike kings, do not serve until they die. They can choose not to run for reelection.

Washington gave a farewell address to the American people. Then he and Martha returned to Mount Vernon in 1797. Once again, he turned his attention to his farm. He was a much older man now and not as strong. One day in December 1799, he was out checking his land. That evening, after a long ride on horseback in the snow and rain, Washington got sick. Two nights later, on December 14, the man known as the father of the United States died at his home. The great war general and the first president was now a part of history. It was up to his country to decide how to honor him.

Building a National Monument

Even while Washington was alive, people wanted to honor him with a monument. In 1783, the Continental Congress decided to honor Washington with a statue. The statue would show him in uniform riding a horse.

Establishing the Capital

The statue would be placed in the new nation's capital, but no one knew where that would be. Philadelphia had been the site of the Continental Congress and the Constitutional Convention. Then, New York City served as the capital. A decision on where to place the capital was finally reached in 1790.

At the time, some of the states could not pay their debts. One of Washington's advisers proposed that the federal government should help the states. The government should pay the debts of states that did not have enough money. Some states in the South, however, had already

This early map of Washington, D.C., made in 1793, shows the planned locations of the White House (center) and the Capitol (right).

paid their debts. They did not want the northern states to get this kind of help. The states reached a compromise in 1790. The federal government would pay the war debts. That was what the northern states wanted. The capital would be moved to a southern location, between Maryland and Virginia, on the banks of the Potomac River. That was what the southern states wanted.

Congress decided to name the new city Washington, after the nation's first president. President Washington chose the exact place for the city, just 16 miles (26 kilometers) north of his home at Mount Vernon. He also chose where his statue would go. It would be on a hill. To the north would be the "President's House." To the east would be "Congress House." (Today, these buildings are called the White House and the Capitol.)

Changing Plans for the Monument

It was more than 100 years before the Washington Monument was finished. What you see today looks nothing like a statue of Washington on a horse.

Washington's Thoughts on a Monument

Why didn't the government build the statue with a horse? The first person who stopped it was Washington. As president, he knew the country had many expenses. He did not think the country should spend money on a statue while he was still alive.

The monument is an **obelisk**. It is a thin, tall four-sided structure of stone that comes to a point at the top.

Plans for the monument changed many times. The first and the last idea, however, have one thing in common. The monument today stands in almost the same location that Washington chose for his statue.

Washington didn't want the statue of him built while he was alive. Then, after Washington died, Congress decided—again—to honor him. This time, Congress wanted to build a **tomb** and put it in the Capitol building. The plan was to put Washington's body in the tomb. Washington, however, was already buried at Mount Vernon. This was what he had asked for before he died. His family refused to go against his wishes. Today, there is a marble tomb for Washington at the Capitol, but it is empty.

The year 1832 marked the 100th anniversary of Washington's birth, but there was still no monument. The members of Congress decided to take action. They gave $5,000 for a statue of Washington. This statue would be made in the style of Greek and Roman art. When the work was finished, people were shocked. The statue showed Washington with a bare chest. He had no clothes on, just a cloth over him. People said it looked like he was "entering a bath." The statue was in the style of Greek and Roman statues, but it was not how Americans wanted to remember the father of their country. The statue was eventually placed in the National Museum of American History. It is still there today.

The Washington National Monument Society

The next year, some government leaders tried something new. They formed a group of citizens. The group was called the Washington National Monument Society. Its job was to raise money for a monument. People were asked to give just one dollar. In three years, the society raised $28,000. This was enough to hold a competition for the monument's design. Many people suggested ideas. The winning design was by the **architect** Robert Mills. He had already created a monument to George Washington in the city of Baltimore, Maryland. His new plan for a

Many people did not like this statue, in the style of Greek and Roman sculpture, that showed Washington wearing just a robe.

national monument was **elaborate**. It called for an obelisk surrounded by a ring of columns. Between the columns were spaces for 30 statues of American heroes. On top of some of the columns would be a platform with a statue of Washington.

Mills's design would cost more than $1 million. The society did not have that much money. It decided to start by building only the obelisk. Maybe later, when it had more money, it would add the columns and the statues.

31

SKETCH OF

WASHINGTON NAT⸗: MONUM⸗:
BY
ROB⸗: MILLS,
ARC⸗.

Architect Robert Mills's plan for the monument included columns surrounding the obelisk.

Mills was not happy with this idea. He said the obelisk alone would look like "a stalk of asparagus."

Work Begins

Congress gave 37 acres (15 hectares) of land to the society. Work began in 1848. The **cornerstone** was laid on July 4. Fifteen thousand people came out to celebrate. There were speeches and lots of cheering. There were fireworks, as well— in honor of the Fourth of July and the monument that was being built.

The society asked for more money while the monument was being built. It asked states, cities, clubs, and individuals. It also asked other countries. It asked anyone who admired Washington to give something. The government of the state of Alabama asked if it could give a building stone instead of money. The society said yes. Then, it invited everyone to give a stone to help build the monument.

In Their Own Words

The Speech of the Day

Robert Winthrop, an important member of Congress, gave the main speech on July 4, 1848, when work on the Washington Monument began. He said the monument showed:

> "the gratitude, not of states, or of cities, or of governments; not of separate communities, or of official bodies; but of the people, the whole people of the nation—a National Monument erected by the citizens of the United States of America."

The Stolen Stone

The donated stones were piled up in a shed on the grounds of the monument. One was donated by Pope Pius IX, the leader of the Roman Catholic Church. All the other stones would one day go inside the monument, but this one disappeared.

The theft took place before sunrise on March 6, 1854, when three men in masks appeared. They attacked the watchman guarding the monument. Then, they found the pope's stone. They lifted it onto a handcart and wheeled it to the edge of the Potomac River. It is assumed they dropped the stone in the river. It was never seen again.

The thieves were from the American Party. (This group was also called the "Know-Nothings.") They did not want **immigrants** to move to the United States. They were also against people who were Catholic. They thought Catholics should not be allowed to give stones to the monument. In 1855, the Know-Nothings held a special election and took control of the Monument Society.

They were not organized enough to raise money, however. The 4 feet (122 centimeters) that were added to the monument while they were in charge were poorly made. They gave up control of the Monument Society after just three years. By then, though, people had lost interest in the project. The public was confused about who was in charge. Congress had taken back the money it was going to give. And the country was on the edge of a **civil war**.

A National Crisis

The states were divided over the issue of slavery. Many in the South thought slavery should be legal. Many in the North thought slavery should be abolished. The disagreement was not new. Washington himself had worried about slavery. He thought the Union between the states might come apart because of it. In his farewell address to the nation, he had asked Americans to think about "the…value of your national union to your…happiness."

People were also thinking about the unity of the United States the day the cornerstone was laid on the Washington Monument. In his speech that day, Robert Winthrop had said that the monument should be "a pledge… of perpetual union."

Such words were not enough to stop the war. In November 1860, Americans elected a new president, Abraham Lincoln. He was against the expansion of slavery into territories that were becoming new states. Before Lincoln was even inaugurated, seven southern states announced they were no longer part of the country. Fighting between the North and South began in April 1861 when southern forces fired on a federal fort, Fort Sumter, in South Carolina. Soldiers from the North surrendered after less than two days of fighting. Soon after, four more southern states seceded. The Civil War had begun.

Stones from Around the World

A total of 193 stones were given for the Washington Monument. Most of the stones were about 2 feet (61 centimeters) high and about 1 foot (30 centimeters) thick. Each stone had a message written on it. Indiana sent a stone that said, "Knows No North, No South, Nothing but the Union." Greece sent a stone calling itself "the Mother of Ancient Liberty." Wales (which is part of Great Britain) sent a stone with a message in Welsh. Translated, it means: "My language, my land, my nation of Wales—Wales forever!" As you can see, some of the messages did not have much to do with the monument.

Two of the stones given for the Washington Monument: above, one from the country of Turkey; right, a stone from the country of Egypt.

BEEF DEPOT MONUM

While the Washington Monument stood unfinished during the Civil War, cattle that would be used to feed the army grazed on the land around it.

No work was done on the monument during the Civil War. Instead, the grounds around it became part of the war effort. A slaughterhouse was set up to provide meat to feed the army. Cattle grazed on the grass. Soldiers from the North practiced there too. The future of the monument—like the future of the country—was uncertain.

The Civil War ended in 1865. The South surrendered, and the 11 southern states rejoined the Union. While the country struggled to recover, the monument was ignored.

The Monument Rises

The year 1876 was an important one. It was the 100th anniversary of the Declaration of Independence. The country had survived the Civil War, which had by then been over for 11 years. It was time to finish the monument. The job of finishing the monument was taken away from the Washington National Monument Society. The United States Army was given the job. An Army engineer was put in charge. His name was Thomas Casey.

It had taken 28 years to build one third of the monument. After Casey and the Army got the job, the project was finished in eight years.

Before they made the monument taller, Casey and his team had to fix problems left by the last crew. They took out the 4 feet (122 centimeters) of work done when the American Party was in control. They also found that the base of the monument was weak. They dug out 70 percent of the ground under the obelisk. Then they put in a stronger base that was made of concrete.

In Their Own Words

"It Is an Eyesore"

Some people were outraged that the monument was left unfinished for so many years. One of them was the writer Mark Twain. He wrote that the stub of the monument looked like a chimney:

> "The ungainly old chimney…is of no…use to anybody…. It may suit the departed George Washington—I don't know. He may think it is pretty. It may be a comfort to him to look at it out of the clouds…but it is not likely…. It is an eyesore to the people. It ought to be either pulled down or built up and finished."

Once the base was secure, the workers were able to build quickly, and they did. By 1884, they came to the final step. They were ready to add the **capstone**. This would have a metal tip to protect the monument from lightning. The material they chose for the tip was aluminum. Not many people had used aluminum. This would be the largest piece ever cast. The Army asked a scientist in Pennsylvania to do the job. He made the tip and sent it to Washington. First, it made a stop in New York City. There, it was displayed in a jewelry store. The aluminum cast was itself a work of art.

The Final Touch

The aluminum tip finally arrived in Washington. It was time to place it on top of the monument. It was a very windy day. People gathered on a platform 550 feet (168 meters) high to watch. The capstone, which weighed 3,300 pounds (1,500 kilograms), had been lifted up with a crane. Now the aluminum tip, which weighed 6¼ pounds (2.8 kilograms), was set in place and connected to a copper rod that passed through the capstone. As it was set, those who watched cheered. The monument was complete.

It took another year before the official dedication. That event was held one day before Washington's birthday: February 21, 1885. As the *New York Times* reported, the winter weather did not stop people from coming.

Egyptian Proportions

The first obelisks were made in Egypt. Usually, the height was 10 times the width of the base. When the Army took over the building of the Washington Monument, the design was changed to fit this model. The height of the monument is 555 feet, 5⅛ inches (169 meters). That is a little more than 10 times the base, which is 55 feet, 1½ inches wide (17 meters).

On a windy day in 1884, as those watching held their hats, the final piece—an aluminum tip—is placed on the top of the monument.

"Despite the cold, intensified by the wind, the seats were quickly filled," said the *Times*. "The remarks of various speakers were inaudible, but the puffs of steam from their mouths was evidence that the proceedings were being carried on according to program." Ohio Senator John Sherman— whose words may or may not have been heard by the crowd—called the monument "a fit memorial to the greatest character in human history."

When the Washington Monument was dedicated, it was the tallest human-made structure in the world. Four years later, the Eiffel Tower in Paris set a new record.

Chapter 5

Visiting the Washington Monument Today

Anyone can visit the Washington Monument. The monument is open every day except July 4 and December 25. Admission is free, but you need to get tickets on the day you are visiting. The monument is a popular place to visit, so it is important to try to get tickets early.

As you wait in line, you can see that the color is different on the upper and lower parts of the monument. This is because work on the monument took place in two main stages. You can see where work stopped and then began again.

Visitors can ride an elevator to the top. There, windows face out in each direction. Looking through the windows, you can get a far-reaching view of Washington, D.C., and beyond. On a clear day, you can see more than 30 miles (48 kilometers).

A View in Every Direction

Looking to the east from the top of the monument, you can see the Capitol building. That is where Congress meets. You can also see the Supreme Court. That is the nation's highest court of law. Looking to the north, you can see the White House. That is where the president lives and works.

Turning to the west, you can see the Lincoln Memorial. This is the nation's tribute to President Abraham Lincoln. There is a pool of water in front of the Lincoln Memorial. You may see the Washington Monument reflected in this water, which is called the Reflecting Pool.

To the south of the Washington Monument is a monument to another great American. This one is for President Thomas Jefferson. Beyond that is the Potomac River. On the far side of the river is the state of Virginia, where George Washington was born. Virginia is also where he is buried today.

As you take the elevator down, you can think about George Washington's life. You can think of how he

Visitors waiting to enter the monument can see that the lower and upper sections, put up at different times, are different colors.

In Their Own Words

A Poem to the Monument

A poem by the American writer Will Carleton was published on the day the monument was dedicated. It is called "At the Summit of the Washington Monument." In one part of the poem, Carleton describes the view to the south:

> Look South! where, in its coat of gray,
> The broad Potomac creeps away,
> And seeks the blue of distant skies;
> But pauses where the great chief lies
> Within his humble, hallowed tomb,
> Amid Mount Vernon's deathless bloom.

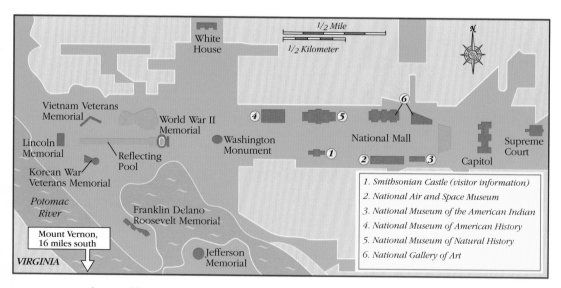

The Washington Monument is one many places of interest to visit in Washington, D.C. Nearby Mount Vernon is also open to visitors.

There are fireworks near the Washington Monument every Fourth of July.

went from a farm boy to a military man to a general and a president. You can also think about the monument. Today, it may be hard to imagine Washington, D.C., without it. However, the monument might have looked completely different. It might never have been finished. There is a fascinating story behind the Washington Monument that is so familiar to Americans today.

Securing the Monument

On September 11, 2001, four airplanes were taken over by **hijackers** and crashed in New York City, Pennsylvania, and just outside Washington, D.C. After this, security got tighter throughout Washington and other places. This was true at the Washington Monument. The U.S. government wanted to protect it from an attack. The government made two changes. It built a low wall around the base. This is to protect the monument from a car being driven into it. It also added metal detectors. These help the staff make sure no one visiting the monument has a hidden weapon. Everyone who visits the monument walks through the metal detectors.

Timeline ★ ★ ★ ★ ★ ★ ★ ★

★ **1732** George Washington is born in Virginia on **February 22**.

★ **1753** Washington becomes a major in Virginia's militia.

★ **1759** Washington marries Martha Custis.

★ **1774** Washington attends the first Continental Congress.

★ **1775** **April:** The first shots are fired in the American Revolution in the battles of Lexington and Concord. **June:** The Continental Congress chooses Washington to be commander in chief of its army.

★ **1776** The Declaration of Independence is written and signed.

★ **1781** Washington's army wins the last major battle of the American Revolution in Yorktown, Virginia.

★ **1783** **September:** The United States and Great Britain sign a peace treaty that recognizes the independence of the United States. **December:** Washington resigns as head of the army and returns to Mount Vernon.

★ **1787** Washington chairs the convention that writes a new constitution for the United States.

★ **1789** Washington becomes the first president of the United States.

★ **1797** Washington returns to Mount Vernon after finishing his second term as president.

★ **1799** Washington dies on **December 14**.

★ **1833** The Washington National Monument Society is formed to raise money for a monument.

★ **1836** Architect Robert Mills wins a competition to design the Washington Monument.

★ **1848** Work begins on a simplified version of Mills's plan.

★ **1876** Thomas Casey and the United States Army are assigned the job of finishing the Washington Monument.

★ **1884** The capstone is placed on top of the monument.

★ **1885** The Washington Monument is officially dedicated on **February 21**.

architect: A person who designs buildings and other structures and who understands how they are built.

capital: The city or town that is the center of a state or country's government.

capstone: The last stone placed on a structure.

civil war: A war between groups within the same country.

colony: An area that is owned and controlled by another country and is not independent.

Congress: The part of the U.S. government that makes the laws.

constitution: A document that outlines a country's or a state's form of government and how laws are made and enforced.

cornerstone: The first stone placed when a structure is being built.

debt: Money or something else that is owed.

elaborate: Detailed and complicated.

estate: A large piece of land with a house on it.

federal: Related to the whole nation, rather than the states.

frontier: An undeveloped area of land on the edge of a settled area.

hijacker: Someone who takes illegal control of a plane or other vehicle.

immigrant: A person who leaves one country to settle in another.

inaugurate: To swear a public official into office.

legislature: The part of a government that makes the laws.

militia: Citizens who train as soldiers and fight when needed.

monument: A structure put up to remember a special person or event.

mourning: Feeling and acting sad because someone has died.

neutrality: Not supporting either side in a conflict.

obelisk: A four-sided pillar made of stone that has a square base and a pointed top.

precedent: An action or decision that guides future actions and decisions.

representative: Someone who speaks or takes action for another person or group of people.

survey: To measure land to find its size and borders.

tomb: A room or building where a person is buried.

To Learn More ★ ★ ★ ★ ★ ★ ★

Read these books

Ashabranner, Brent K. *The Washington Monument: A Beacon for America*. Brookfield, Conn.: Twenty-first Century Books, 2002.

Calkhoven, Laurie. *George Washington: An American Life*. New York: Sterling Publishing, 2007.

Curlee, Lynn. *Capital*. New York: Atheneum, 2003.

Dolan, Edward F. *George Washington*. New York: Marshall Cavendish Benchmark, 2008.

Hort, Lenny. *George Washington: A Photographic Story of a Life*. New York: DK Publishing, 2005.

Marcovitz, Hal. *The Washington Monument*. Philadelphia: Mason Crest Publishers, 2003

Look up these Web sites

Biography of George Washington
http://www.whitehouse.gov/history/presidents/gw1.html

Mount Vernon
http://www.mountvernon.org

National Park Service, National Register of Historic Places—Washington Monument
http://www.nps.gov/history/nr/travel/wash/dc72.htm

National Park Service—Washington Monument
http://www.nps.gov/wamo

Papers of George Washington: Learning about George Washington
http://gwpapers.virginia.edu/education/kids/teacherintro.html

Key Internet search terms

American Revolution, Thomas Casey, Continental Congress, Constitutional Convention, French and Indian War, George Washington, Mount Vernon, Washington Monument, Washington, D.C.

★ ★ ★ ★ ★ ★ ★ ★ ★ Index

The abbreviation *ill.* stands for illustration, and *ills.* stands for illustrations. Page references to illustrations and maps are in *italic* type.

Index ★ ★ ★ ★ ★ ★ ★ ★ ★ ★

★ ★

About the Author

Julia Schaffer has written several books for young people. They include *Isabel's Story, The Elephant in the Room*, and *St. Louis: Gateway to the West*. She first visited the Washington Monument when she was 16 years old. She can still picture the way the monument looked at sunset. Julia lives and works in New York City.